I0445317

REIGNITING YOUR IMPACT

Actionable Strategies for Overcoming

Leadership Setbacks and Defeat

Dr. Keena R. Mosley

ISBN: 979-8-9872482-0-1 (Paperback)
ISBN: 979-8-9872482-1-8 (Ebook)
Library of Congress Control Number: 2022920790

Because of the dynamic nature of the internet, any web addresses or links contained in this book may have changed since publication and may no longer be valid. The views expressed in this work are solely those of the author and do not necessarily reflect the views of the publisher, and the publisher disclaims any responsibility for them.

Printed in the United States of America

Visit www.myimpactbook.com/tools

For free tools to help you reignite your impact

DEDICATION

This book is dedicated to my mother for making sure that we knew how to work hard and never quit, to the village that showed me how to recover and to my support system that keeps me going.

Thank you all for dusting me off again and again.

TABLE OF CONTENTS

ACKNOWLEDGEMENT

Jasmine Womack and the Empact University Team you are an incredible group of people to whom I am forever grateful.

INTRODUCTION

In flight school, pilots are taught to warn passengers of danger by saying "brace for impact." I can't tell you how many times that I wished there was a brace for impact announcement in my actual life. If I could, I would give everyone in my reach a warning, but it just isn't always possible. What is possible is to make sure that you have the tools to get unstuck when you face a setback or defeat. This book is designed to give you actionable strategies that stop the downward spiral that can occur when things don't go well in your professional life. If you are navigating a career setback, have experienced a significant defeat, or are feeling stifled by your workplace, this book is for you. This book is going to provide you with the steps needed to get out of your dark place.

I know exactly where you are because I have been there more than once. Yes, I have been in a place that felt like the end of the road. There were days when I literally felt under attack. I felt disrespected, ignored, and rejected. Fortunately, the toxic work environment in which I found myself didn't overtake me. Instead, I was able to overcome the challenges placed before me, and I was able to get my fire back. It wasn't an overnight success, but I worked hard, and because of these strategies, I was able to build a strong team, turn around some significant organizational challenges, and eventually launch my own company.

With over 30 years of experience in early education, nonprofit, and social services sectors, I have been able to accelerate organizational performance and help teams experience lasting success. During a time when I could have easily given up, I decided that I was not going to give in to the toxicity I experienced, and I had to stop believing what others were projecting onto me. Once I took control of myself and employed the strategies outlined in this book, I saw significant growth, both personally and professionally. My team was able to exceed organizational goals. I launched new initiatives and ultimately gave birth to my dream.

Despite the obstacles you may have encountered in your career or the challenges you may be facing currently, this doesn't have to be the end of your journey. Nor does it need to be the end of your team's success. This book is designed to help you reclaim your influence, engage your team at optimal levels and take full authority over your leadership legacy. It won't be easy, and it won't happen overnight, but I do know that the strategies will work - if you work them. You deserve to have a reputation which you can be proud, and you absolutely can have it! I look forward to seeing you in the winners' circle!

REFLECTION IS REQUIRED

Your thoughts control more of you than you admit. Manage your thoughts, and you can empower your actions. Empowered actions lead to elevated lives.

Go online to download the
Impact Reflection Guide

www.myimpactbook.com/tools

CHAPTER 1

Get to the Bottom of It

When everything seems to be going against you, remember that the airplane takes off against the wind, not with it.
- Henry Ford

grew up in a very involved and very connected extended family. I have lots of cousins, aunts, and uncles who would spend time together during holidays, weekends, and special events. I was fortunate enough to have one cousin who is just a couple of months younger than me. As a result, he and I probably spent more time together than any of the cousins combined. This also afforded me the opportunity to spend a lot of time with his parents. His father, my uncle, was a man of very few words, but when he spoke, we had to listen. One of his regular sayings was, "You need to nip that in the bud." Naively, I thought when he meant that we should stop doing something. As an adult, I now realize that there was so much more to the statement, and it has become a life philosophy of mine. When he said, "You need to nip it in the bud," what he meant was that you need to get to the bottom of the situation, so it doesn't occur again. You need to get past what's happening on the surface and address the core issue. I get that now. I didn't understand that then, but as a result of understanding how powerful and how important that is, it has become a way of life for me. Unfortunately, depending on how sensitive or emotional a situation is, I tend to lose sight of this very important philosophy. One significant time that I lost sight of it was when I was in what some would call a very toxic work environment.

Twenty-five years into my career as an educator and 16 years as an educational leader, nipping it in the bud neither was at the forefront of my thoughts nor was it informing my decisions. At that point, I was proud of my accomplishments and felt good about how I had progressed professionally. I was the person who had awards, recognitions, invitations, and degrees, and I could not believe that this was happening to me. I had 16 years of making a difference, supporting others, and winning. I had sixteen years of innovation and challenging limitations, 16 years of exceeding expectations and being a trusted adviser, and 16 years of being respected as a leader with whom other leaders confided, but here I was sitting in a rocking chair as a babysitter, literally questioning my professional existence and wondering if somehow it had been a fluke. Suddenly, I realized that this wasn't what I signed up for.

The Setback

I thought I was going to be a part of a stellar team of leaders who skillfully and strategically worked together to create something phenomenal, but that wasn't the case at all. Instead of being a part of a phenomenal team, just the opposite seemed to happen, and I couldn't have seen what was coming. I didn't count on having my scope of responsibility decimated to the point where I was what now seemed like a distant memory. In the blink of an eye, I was stripped of any authority and 97% of my responsibility (yes, I calculated it) for reasons that may never be known to me. My administrative door key had even been taken! Colleagues were dismissive, and they seemingly were empowered to treat me like a complete misfit. I was shaken to my core. It was a painful and humbling time. Rejection and depression took their toll, and worry and sickness became constant companions. After seeking counseling, I realized that the problem wasn't as much about what was happening around me. The biggest issue was that I had bought into what others were projecting on me. At that point, my failures were no longer about what others were saying or doing, but they were about my mindset, and that belief was the route I needed to correct. The belief that I had adopted unwittingly was what I needed to eliminate. That belief was what I needed to nip in the bud. I had completely lost sight of who I really was, and all that it took to get to where I was.

Many years before this setback, I moved completely across the country to forge my own path and create my own place in the world. As a young woman, who was alone without much money and without any relocation plan or assistance, I made it happen. I found a job. I got my first apartment along with earning new credentials. I went back to school for advanced degrees and simultaneously had an amazing career full of upward progress. I even purchased my first home. All of that took courage. It took bravery. It took planning. It took strategy. It took enormous effort that suddenly seemed to disappear, but it hadn't. I had just ignored it. I lost sight of who I was and what I was capable of doing. I was capable of reinventing myself. I was capable of starting over. I was capable of building and climbing, and improving myself, and I was capable of nurturing relationships and forging partnerships and collaborations. This experience could only be a temporary setback because at that point, I refused to let it be anything else. I was determined to move forward at that point. I decided that was not how my story was going to end. That was not going to be my leadership legacy.

The Defeat

Fast forward a bit. All of the toxic decision makers were no longer associated with the organization, and the new leadership enabled us to make some incredible strides with the organization. My name had been cleared. My reputation was restored, and my authority was elevated. Several of the initiatives that I previously suggested were in place, which caused the organization to soar. Despite the success, the organization lost a significant source of funding, and three years after my setback began, we experienced what I perceived to be a significant defeat. Programmatically, the organization needed to make some significant shifts. Personally, I was in a very new place. I received a layoff notice, and I wondered what my next steps would be. As I consoled staff, supported community members, informed clients, and connected with transition agencies, I questioned myself once again. This time, the questions were different. This time I was more sure of myself, but I was unaware of how to recover from this defeat. I was literally at the peak of my career, and suddenly, the bottom fell out. I was also physically, emotionally, and mentally exhausted, and I shuddered to think how I was going to replace my six-figure salary.

Whether it was a setback or a defeat, one thing that I have learned is that leadership is born out of who you are and shaped by what you do. Your thoughts affect how you show up, and what you believe is critical to how you address your staff, how you make decisions, and how you move forward in your day-to-day responsibilities. Just as you have been responsible for your success, you also have to realize that you have some responsibility for your failure. I was definitely responsible for the decision to be held hostage by my failure. Maybe you can relate. Maybe you are in a place where a career altering setback or defeat feels like weights around your ankles and you feel incapable of moving forward. Nonetheless, no matter what is going on around you, your environment doesn't have to dictate your level of success. Each one of us has access to everything we need. That access may look different depending on where we are and who we are. Having access doesn't mean that what you need is in your immediate grasp. What it means is that you have a variety of things at your disposal or that somehow are connected to you. You have access to the internet, social media, current contacts, resources, and other people who also have all these things. This access will allow you to get to your next stage and ultimately, it will help you discover whatever your final destination is. Yes, I do believe you have access to everything you need. Sometimes, you just have to unearth those things and discover where the access point is.

Getting to the root of whatever slump you're in is the only way to identify a path to reclaiming your strength and ultimately, your impact. The mental and emotional toll of a defeat must be tempered, so it does not destroy what you are building going forward. This is the time when your mindset matters most. You can't build well on a faulty foundation. Over time, cracks will begin to surface. You hold the key to your deliverance. You hold the key to your freedom. You hold the key to your next round of success and accomplishments. You have to decide that you want more, and you are worthy of more. Once you decide to get over the hump, and once you decide to get out of the slump, you can take charge of the situation and get to whatever it is that you were created and designed to do.

Reflection

1. Why are you on this career path? Why have you stayed?

2. What is at the core of the setback?

3. Why did you buy into that diminished your excitement, your energy, your passion or your drive?

4. What needs to happen for you to implement the action items listed below?

Action Items

1. Reflect on where you are and the impact it has had on you. Acknowledge your disappointment and its true source. Be sure to determine if you have bought into beliefs or behaviors that are counterintuitive to your core values or characteristics.

2. Identify the things that are holding you back and deal with them. Once you know the source of your constraint, you can work to overcome it.

3. Commit to rising above what is happening around you. Your environment is not nearly as important as what you bring to the table.

Evaluation

1. How effective was your implementation of the action items?

2. What more can be done?

3. Is there a more excellent way?

_____

_____

_____

_____

_____

_____

_____

_____

_____

_____

_____

_____

**LEADERSHIP IS BORN OUT OF
WHO YOU ARE AND SHAPED BY
WHAT YOU DO.**

PROGRESS OVER PASSIVITY

You are the change agent that your world is in need of.

It's time to show up...

Go online to download the
Momentum Magnifier

www.myimpactbook.com/tools

CHAPTER 2

Respect Your Influence

Leadership is no longer about your position. It's now more about your passion for excellence and making a difference. You can lead without a title.

\- Robin Sharma

I t has been said that influence is the true measure of leadership. Theorists will tell us that there are different types of leadership. When you have influence, you are followed because of the impact you have. You are respected because of thoughts around who you are and what you do and because of how you have shaped the work, lives, or community for others. Leaders' authority is based on reputation, relationship, and transformative impact. Positional leadership causes people to go along with your direction, your vision, and your ideas because the position you are in dictates such. Likewise, managers often are operating from a position on a chart/diagram. It is authority based on the role they play in an organization. Ultimately, a position doesn't guarantee influence; it only grants a measure of authority. As a result, it is quite possible to have a position but no influence, which leaves you with only a semblance of power. This kind of power if not handled properly can be dangerous. The type of leadership we are focused on in this book is beyond a position. Our attention is on influence and the transformation that occurs when others have respect and regard for not just what you do, but for who you are and the results that you produce.

Influential leadership expands beyond the title you hold, the badge you wear, the office you occupy, or the seat in which you sit. My journey with the organization where I had the setback began as a consulting gig for a staff training. I spent two full days with the majority of their staff providing guidance on the completion of a state requirement. Over those two days, I would say about 25% of the staff approached me at one point or another about an executive-level vacancy that just opened. Somehow, they thought I would be an excellent choice to fill that position. At the time, I didn't know anything about the opening or the history of the vacancy. I knew a little bit about the organization. What I knew about the organization was more than most might know, but certainly it was not enough information to consider myself to be a part of the inner workings of their operations. However, I did have some knowledge of who they were, what they were about, and what their situation was. I knew that there were going to be some challenges. Despite their recent turmoil, my influence shone through with no intentional effort of my own. The staff had no knowledge of me yet, over those two days, they really did their best to sell me on why I was a good fit for them. They really wanted me to join them. I realized that they weren't necessarily attracted to me per se. What they were attracted to were the things they were hungry for in leadership. They were looking for knowledge and for a commitment to excellence. They wanted someone to push them to grow. They wanted relatability, and they wanted someone who could be firm with them but could also be kind, and apparently, they saw those things in me. As a point of clarity, my decision to pursue this opportunity was made based on my relationship with a member of the executive team and an invitation by decision makers.

Reflecting on this situation and the way I started my journey with them, one thing I've learned is that it's important to embrace the things that have led to your success. Knowing the core values, innate strengths, and track record that propel and have propelled you thus far is critical. As you are reigniting your impact, you have to approach this time as a reboot. You have to know where you came from, and you have to understand the foundation on which you stand because allowing yourself to be put in a box, paralyzed, and held hostage by setbacks and defeats will cause you to lose touch with your core. It will cause you to have professional amnesia, but you need to remember how you got to this place. In times of defeat, it's important to remember that greatness begets greatness. When you rebuild on the foundation of what you did well, you have a greater chance of success. Focusing on failure alone only brings more disappointment, shame, and regret. To avoid making this defeat your lasting legacy, you must bring your accomplishments to the forefront of your thoughts.

Although it has almost become a cliché, knowing who you are as well as why you have chosen this path are necessary components. When you blend your success and influence with your why, you have results. When you blend your influence with your why, you can have clarity on how you are to move forward, and that is what will lead to future accomplishments. Start with the person in the mirror. You have to start with leading yourself, and you have to buy into who you are before others can jump on your bandwagon completely. Both you and those you lead have to believe that you can produce when it matters most. Use influence instead of position.

Not only do people follow leaders who are stronger than them, but they also mimic what they see. It's important to use past and current success as a launching point for overcoming setbacks and defeats. If you want to know how leaders are doing, you look for their impact on their followers. People join an organization for the work/the mission (or other factors), but they most often choose to stay or decide to leave because of leaders. They make decisions about level of commitment and continuance because of the people with whom they are associated. Every message people receive is filtered through the messenger. This means if they don't trust or respect you as their leader, they barely are listening to you. Every exchange that they have with you becomes one of obligation, and their response is going to be driven by what they perceive in you. Gone are the days when respect is earned simply because of a title. Your influence exudes without a corner office, without your name on a door, or absent of an elevated title. People will always respond to how you make them feel so make them feel valued, respected, seen, and appreciated. Do these things, and you will have their attention.

Reflection

1. Are you a leader whom others will follow? Are you a leader whom you will follow?

2. If your career ended today, and speeches were made about you, what do you hope they would say about you as a leader?

3. What characteristics, beliefs, and values helped you to become who you are?

4. Who are you influencing and how?

5. What do you need to do to become the leader you hope to be?

6. What needs to happen for you to implement the action items listed below?

Action Items

1. Identify your results and make a list of your accomplishments. Reflecting on your accomplishments isn't for others. It is to remind you of what you are capable of doing.

2. Let others do the talking while you keep doing the work. Be a leader who others want to follow, and you will never have to prove your authority. If you sparingly share your track record as a story or example, it doesn't feel like bragging or being boastful.

3. Identify the places within your control where your expertise is needed. These are the places where you can begin making an impact.

4. Acknowledge your team for their contributions. Every employee has done something to improve the organization, the team, or you individually. Tell them that you noticed.

Evaluation

1. How effective was your implementation of the action items?

2. What more can be done?

3. Is there a more excellent way?

"

USE INFLUENCE
INSTEAD OF POSITION.

CHAPTER 3

Build Momentum

Effective leadership is not about making speeches or being liked. Leadership is defined by results and attributes.
- Peter Drucker.

Do you remember that childhood story about a little train that was trying to go up a mountain but wasn't really sure if he could? He kept looking at this mountain, and eventually, he willed himself into making the climb. Inch by inch and yard by yard, the train built momentum. Know that when you are building momentum, it's just like that train. It's that forward movement that you're experiencing continually. Momentum is a series of moments. It's a series of small steps. It's the repetition and the daily practices that build up to be a great force. When most people think of momentum, they think of a huge force, but momentum is built over time. Momentum is built with effort.

I was that train. I was the train that was trying to climb up what seemed like an insurmountable mountain. While I was trying to get out of my hole, I had to push myself one step, one decision, one victory, and one moment at a time. When I was assigned to a small and seemingly insignificant portion of the organization, what was said to me was, "I'm giving this to you, and you can do what you want with it. It's yours to blow, and if you blow it, it's all on you." A folder was thrown on my desk, and then the person made a quick exit.

This was an isolated department that was void of support, and unbeknownst to me, it was managed improperly from its launch. It was not just mine to blow, it also now was mine to correct. On the surface, things looked pretty bad, but I saw an opportunity, and I was determined to make the best of this situation and do what no one expected. What they didn't know was that when you tell me it's all on me, I believe and behave like it's all on me. When you tell me that is mine to blow, I take that as a full challenge, and I am going to show you exactly how to make a miracle happen.

After a couple of weeks of making a few seemingly impossible things happen, my little team of four came to me with a few confessions. They admitted to needing more support and shared that they did not have the needed information and resources to perform as expected. They also told me that initially, they were apprehensive of having to report to me but were now glad that they were working with me because I got things done for them. In that same conversation, they committed to doing anything necessary to right-side this department, and they said they were ready to go full steam ahead. This is what building momentum looks like.

You have to start moving, and you have to get things going in the right direction. When you are refocusing, re-claiming, and rebuilding, little progress is far better than no progress at all. Motion builds momentum. Motion creates action, and action is what drives momentum. Just like the rotations of the train wheels, building momentum is cycli-cal. The more movement you have, the more momentum is generated, and the more momentum that is generated, the more movement you have. Productive movement and momentum look like achieving goals, fresh ideas, innovative systems, and victories that were once unimaginable, are now all within reach. A perfect way to do that is to build on your past success and the success of the team. Nothing at all speaks like a good track record. Followers trust leaders with a good track record. Trust is the foundation of leadership and people both follow and buy into leaders who can get things done.

You can build trust by being consistent, demonstrating competence, having good character, and having concern or connection with those you lead. If you want people to follow you confidently, they need to see results, and they need to know that you are there for them in a real and tangible way.

Stack wins, keep score, and help them realize that they also help you win. That's when the idea of the team really sets in, and the momentum really starts to build. Find a way both make things happen for them and make decisions strategically. Focus on their needs and not on yours. Your decision should be based on the good of others and not yourself. You have to remember that people expect their leaders to help them achieve their goals, (even if they never say it) which ultimately empowers them. When you are empowering others, you give yourself more power by giving your power away. As you empower your team, not only do you have the power, effort, and energy you possess, you now have all of their skills and resources behind you as well. When you help team members achieve their goals, they'll help you achieve yours. However, if you don't empower others, and you don't help them reach their goals, you end up creating a barrier. Barriers cause people to give up or go away, but if your team knows you are a winner, and you want them to win, they will want you to win too.

One of the core foundations of human development and psychology is Abraham Maslow's Hierarchy of Needs. He explains that we are driven by five essential areas of need which are pooled together in two major categories – deficiency needs and growth needs. The deficiency needs motivate us based on their absence. We are driven to reduce the unpleasant reality of their absence. These deficiency needs are related to our basic needs being met including safety, health, relationships, and connection. Growth needs motivate us based on their presence. We are driven to increase the fulfillment in these areas as we attain more. These growth needs are related to success, self-esteem, freedom, and respect. The needs are built on the strength of each other. When our deficiency needs are met, we are more equipped to perform to fulfill our growth needs. Once there is a disruption to any of our needs, the other needs are affected as well. This is key to understanding how to build momentum with team members. We all have a desire to succeed, but there may be a need to address deficiency needs before asking more of someone. In instances in which someone has had a measure of success, failure of any sort must be viewed as a means of promoting forward movement. If not, that failure can quickly impede progress because it becomes a threat to deficiency needs. Instead of searching for more success, human nature seeks out a place of acceptance, not more success. The remedy for this is continuous movement.

You're going to boost your performance with continuous movement and continued success. As much as leadership is about influence, it is also about results, and if your influence doesn't lead to some sort of result, then what are you doing? Every leader must have a track record of success. The higher and more important your influence, the more important your track record becomes. If you aren't responsible for the progress of others as a leader, are you really leading? As a result of being laid off, I was devastated, but eventually, I realized that the shame I felt came from my own internal struggle. Funding losses and changes are not uncommon occurrences in the nonprofit sector, so what I needed to do was reframe my thinking. The acknowledgment of your defeat is necessary but not nearly as much as the acknowledgment of the lessons learned. Now is the time to begin charting your next steps from an informed place. You must give yourself permission to take calculated risks and identify the potential roadblocks along the way. Here is where you identify what you aspire to do and the results you desire to have. Somehow, my emotional intelligence was fully present for everyone except myself. Many times, what we see as a defeat is simply a rerouting. As you wrestle with your defeat, perhaps it is time for you to take a new direction, and this latest disappointment is the lane change that you needed.

Reflection

1. What has been your biggest accomplishment, and why is it important to you?

2. What are some things that you can do to get some quick, yet meaningful wins?

3. What does your team need most, and how can you begin to address that void?

4. What needs to happen for you to implement the action items listed below?

_____

_____

_____

_____

_____

_____

_____

_____

Action Items

1. Consider what things can be addressed quickly and succinctly. This will begin to provide direction and ignite momentum-building confidence.

2. Determine potential obstacles and commit to moving forward. Slow movement is better than no movement, and eventually, no movement turns to regression.

3. Create wins. Your team's success equals your success, and it will serve you well. In times of defeat, you will need to identify ways that you can win.

Evaluation

1. How effective was your implementation of the action items?

2. What more can be done?

3. Is there a more excellent way?

_____

_____

_____

_____

_____

_____

_____

_____

_____

_____

_____

_____

FOLLOWERS TRUST LEADERS WITH A GOOD TRACK RECORD.

FORWARD FACING MOVEMENT

Your past is proof of potential, but your future is calling ahead.

The choice is yours.

Go online to download the
Problem Solving Matrix and Meeting Agenda

www.myimpactbook.com/tools

CHAPTER 4

Solve Their Problems (and Yours too)

Leadership is solving problems. The day soldiers stop bringing you their problems is the day you have stopped leading them. They have either lost confidence that you can help or concluded that you do not care. Either case is a failure of leadership.

- Colin Powell.

I love crime shows and mysteries. It is exhilarating to get to the bottom of whodunit. In order to uncover all the clues, you need to pull information from a vacuum, be diligent in your quest, and piece together all of the variables. I've often been told that I could make a living as a private investigator. Somehow, a leader solving problems in the real world doesn't provide the same type of adrenaline boost. However, it is one of the most important things that you can do to gain trust and contribute to a positive culture.

In order to solve problems and get to the bottom of things, I had to do a lot of listening. I listened to the complaints, and I listened to the concerns, I listened to and reviewed the data, and then I was able to present both solutions to problems that plagued the program for years and offer a measure of innovation. This success was attributed to my persistence in digging to uncover the needed information, talking to team members on different levels, and using every opportunity possible to get to the bottom of what the problems really were. You see, I conducted a root cause analysis on just about everything I did and about every complaint that came to me. As leaders, we have to realize that at the core of every complaint that is brought to our attention is a problem that needs to be solved - a need that must be addressed. If you want to reclaim your impact, identify the problems and dig deeply to resolve them. Don't settle for just resolving the surface issues. Get enough information to address the root cause and engage others, so they can become a part of the solution.

Uncover and Identify

The problems that you are required to solve are most often complex with multiple layers. Your team sees the surface of the issue, but when you dig more deeply, you easily can determine that it's more than meets the eye. In order to determine where all of the problems are, a root-cause analysis is necessary. On the surface of every problem is a symptom and visible problem. If you settle for addressing these things, it is a short-lived victory, and the problem along with related symptoms will continue to plague you. A root-cause analysis will cause you to go beyond the superficial cause and effect symptoms by focusing on why and how something occurred.

In my newly assigned department, there was a constant issue with meeting enrollment numbers. As soon as the workers had a full caseload, a child would age out and need to be transitioned to the program for the next age range. There was a time constraint on how long teachers could have an open spot without it causing compliance issues for the program. On the surface, it looked like the workers were missing deadlines and not filling vacancies. The analysis revealed that the strategy for enrollment and recruitment prioritized older children over younger children. This priority ranking was literally the cause of the revolving door. Once this was changed, the revolving door was reduced dramatically. Workers were challenged with meeting timelines because they had limited time to both recruit new families and meet with families to complete the enrollment process. We needed to build a pool of families who were familiar with us and positioned to complete the enrollment process. This was accomplished by starting recruitment from the pool of existing preschool families. Recruitment materials were updated to represent all program options, so parents were informed of what was available to them. The team that was assigned to enroll preschool families were now inquiring about the younger children in the household and initiating the process to add these children to the waiting list. These steps nearly erased the problems. The symptom of the problem looked like employees missing requirements and focusing on this in isolation was not yielding the needed results. It was a root-cause analysis that uncovered the systems' problems. This quest to get to the bottom of the problem identified who needed to be involved in the solution and help us to define how the final outcome should look. Initially, team members were both weary and leary when I started asking questions, but I reassured them that my questions were a quest to elim-inate their problems. The more problems that were solved, the more answers I would get. The unexpected benefit of this approach was that they started handling problems the same way. Before they came to me with a problem, they analyzed as much as they could, and our discussions would start with the things that they had already uncovered! It also evolved into me asking for their recommendations.

Decisions are best made with informed input from others, but if you are making decisions as a party of one, you need to be sure to weigh the pros and cons of varied approaches. When working with others, you should always ask for their input. Contributing to a resolution is much more empowering than receiving a resolution. In order to continue moving forward and solve problems for yourself and others, coordinated communication between overlapping or aligned areas allows you to reduce new problems and bottlenecks while increasing efficiency, effectiveness, and innovation. Involving team members from varied levels and positions allows you to solve problems with a more effective and comprehensive perspective. Variety does not always mean a larger quantity. Involving too many people can slow down your progress. What you want most are the people with a diversity in their depth and a breadth of relevant information. However you engage in this process, be sure to think about how this solves your immediate issue and how it might impact other areas in the future. The idea is to implement solutions that will have a positive impact beyond this moment. Leaders have the unique challenge of looking to the future while communicating in the present. As a result, it is important to think of the big picture and specific circumstances. Once the resolution is reached it must be communicated to all who are involved directly and those who are observing on the perimeter. This communication should include the problem, solution, and levels of responsibility.

Assign and Evaluate

Someone must be specifically responsible for every aspect of the solution. If you give it any measure of thought, you probably can recall when you have participated in a discussion in which there were great ideas shared with big goals. Eventually, nothing became of this creative energy because the ideas never transitioned to an actual plan with identified parties, deadlines, and any information related to the how of the tasks. The resolution conversation is not over until there is someone responsible for every facet of the next steps. Every task needs a name and a deadline. Once these things are in place, you are ready to take action, but this is not where it ends. After a period of time, it is necessary to determine if things are going as they should - analyze, observe, review. Did it work? Did it get to where you need it to be? Did you correctly identify your outcome?

When you fail to evaluate, you may end up in the same place, or you may have a new problem that you have to address that currently is lying dormant. Checking in also communicates that you remain open and available. Strong leaders demonstrate a willingness to openly support and promote the needs within their realm of influence. You can't impact everything. You can't touch and be responsible for everything, but for the things you can touch and for the things for which you can be responsible, those are the areas you need to handle masterfully.

Problem solving efforts always should be forward facing. You want to listen, and you want to look ahead to position yourself for progress. You want to hear what team members are saying and get down to the core of what it is that they're trying to communicate. Despite a lack of exposure, a lack of resources, or a lack of knowledge, their experience is no less valid. Sometimes, team members just don't have the ability to solve their own problems, which makes it the responsibility of the leader to take care of those things. Unless you are very intentional while serving as a leader, it is easy to overlook your accomplishments. As my team entered the closing transition, our conversations began to shift to a place where we reviewed the things that we had done well. This was helpful for my team because it was a way of preparing for interviews. It was effective for me because it reminded me of the problems that I was positioned to solve again. This type of reflective discourse can be both motivating and informative. Your focus cannot be solely on the current moment. You always need to solve problems with the future in mind. Is this solution going to be sustainable? Is this solution going to position us for continued growth, continued expansion, and sustainability? If you solve problems, you lessen people's anxiety about problems, and you also reduce the occurrence of further problems both now and in the future. A leader who solves problems is a leader who builds trust.

Reflection

1. What solutions do you bring to your area of influence?

2. What processes are you willing to confront or adapt to increase performance and reduce barriers?

3. What needs to happen for you to implement the action items listed below?

Action Items

Note: If you are embarking on a new journey, these should still be completed to identify ways to avoid similar problems as you move forward.

1. List your top 5 problems and conduct a root cause analysis. The true solution is often buried beneath the symptoms. Failure to acknowledge this will result in recurring issues.

2. Identify your problem-solving team. The more perspectives you have involved the more informed your decision can be. Be sure to maximize strengths and interests.

3. Use problems as opportunities for growth and innovation. Oftentimes, a pain point is the key to the solution. Those who are most frustrated can tell you passionately what that pain is.

Evaluation

1. How effective was your implementation of the action items?

2. What more can be done?

3. Is there a more excellent way?

"

A LEADER WHO SOLVES PROBLEMS IS A LEADER WHO BUILDS TRUST.

CHAPTER 5

Take and Apply Accountability

Criticism may not be agreeable, but it is necessary. It fulfills the same function as pain in the human body. It calls attention to an unhealthy state of things.
- Winston Churchill.

have never met anyone who enjoys the performance evaluation process. It tends to be routine drudgery that is demanded by a long-standing policy or contract. Part of the problem is that it occurs at a predetermined, yet isolated point in time. This process is such a burden that many companies are revamping their framework regarding employee performance. What they're finding is that routine check-ins are much more valuable than just having an annual review. In fact, companies report that:

- Employees are three times more engaged when they receive daily feedback from their managers versus annual feedback.

- Highly engaged employees are 87% less likely to leave their roles.

- 92% of employees want feedback more than just once a year.

- 77% of human resource leaders say the annual reviews are not an accurate representation of employees' work.

One of the things I know for certain is that employees don't like surprises in their evaluations. If you have gotten to the point in an annual evaluation where the content is surprising to the person on the other side of your desk, then you haven't done your job. The other faulty thing in the evaluation process is the evaluation of leaders. As leaders, we often are watching what our subordinates are doing, but who's watching the leader?

Leaders tend to be great at holding others accountable for their actions or worse, their inactions. However, leaders are rarely good at being held accountable and letting others know about their own missteps. What leaders do instead is self-correct in such a way that others never have a chance to notice exactly what went wrong. This was something I learned to correct over time. When I went through my setback, I would do what worked well for me in the past. As a former classroom teacher (who had to work alone) and someone who had regard and respect for deadlines, I learned to tunnel into my work. I am one of those people who can get into a zone and stay there. This approach didn't work in my executive team position, and it didn't work for my leaders. When I would go into my office, close the door, tunnel into the work, and get into my zone, it seemed to them that I was separating myself from others. It appeared as if I wasn't being a team player. To me, the closed door meant I needed to focus, and I also communicated to them, "Please knock if you need me." It was the exact message that I shared with others. To my leaders, the closed door communicated something different. It said, "You can't come in. I don't want to be bothered." That was a cultural norm that I needed to understand and respect. Instead, I trusted a faulty history and didn't acknowledge how the relationship I had with other team members had changed. I misread a lot of things over time. I ignored the small fires, both the little things people said were bothering them and the little things that bothered me. I thought maybe they would correct themselves. I thought they were going to go away. I thought they were maybe one-offs. Instead, there was an inferno building, and I completely missed it.

I needed to temper myself and communicate better. By tempering myself, I don't mean I was walking around with a bad attitude or anything, but I needed to understand what was going on around me and change my temperament to adapt to those circumstances and my environment. I'm pretty even keeled, and I was the same person all the time. I am who I am everywhere I go, and it typically takes a lot to ruffle my feathers. Even when my feathers are ruffled, you may not know that, and in this situation, the "never let 'em see you sweat" approach was not effective. My steadiness was misread as apathy. My steadiness was misread as being with-drawn particularly when you add my tunneled-in workstyle and the fact that I did not communicate as much as others thought necessary. They didn't understand me. I saw the same fires and concerns that they saw, and that's why I was working so hard (in my office). Instead, what they expected was a level of intensity like those who came before me. An-other thing I learned was that to whom much responsibility is given, much responsibility is required. Because of this, all the things that I've mentioned also needed to be addressed and adapted, but I missed it, and I messed up. The principal thing is that as a leader, you have to take ownership of your crap. When things don't go well, the number one way to re-bound is by taking ownership, apologizing, communicating, and figuring out the next best steps with yourself and others. I revised my approach to accountability by including one-on-one meetings with my supervisor, one-on-one meetings with individual team members, and group meetings with my full team. Team meetings were the time when we would talk together about department-related matters, trends, goals, etc. One-on-one meetings were focused on individual topics and their specific responsibilities.

My biggest adjustment was scheduling regular check-in meetings with my leader, and when my leader chose not to meet with me, I sent emails. If I was out for more than a couple of hours, I would check in after the absence just to make sure that I was still in tune with what was going on and had not missed anything pressing. I scheduled weekly meetings with my leader and made sure to cover specific things each time. The start of the conversation was focused on my current assignments and an update on my progress. It was the lesson learned from tunneling in. I took accountability for the disconnect and actively engaged in ways to bridge the gap. From there, I moved into what was going well, what the challenges were that I was having, and where I needed further guidance. Sharing the challenges and needs for guidance helped to showcase my problem-solving skills and eliminate surprises. Most leaders are not amiable to surprises, and the higher up you go, the less desirable a surprise is. It provided the opportunity to place something on my leader's radar and perhaps indicate where assistance or collaboration may be necessary. I included the things that were going well and the things that were coming up. This was how I highlighted some of my strengths, accomplishments, and strategic planning efforts. The environment in which I worked was compliance-driven, used a bit of a deficit model, and had lots of deadlines and regulations. Respectively, it was very important to be able to communicate that strategic planning was always on my radar, and it was something I used to manage my time and my responsibilities. Last but certainly not least, I would ask my leader, "What would you like to see from me?" This was the time I would give my leader to find out if there was something to be assigned to me based on everything I shared and based on what was going on in my sphere. I also asked, "Is there something you want to assign to me? Is there something you see as problematic? As the one who is being led, I, too, am not a fan of surprises from my leader." Usually, subordinates can take surprises from everywhere else. When it comes from a leader, it feels very unsafe. Being able to open this conversation was very necessary for me to prepare myself as much as possible and to create my own shield of protection.

What I ultimately realized was that this strategy wasn't

just good for when I had conversations with my leader, but these were strategies that I needed to have when I was working with my team. It was very important for me to work with my team who needed a lot of support to call them up and not call them out. Let me explain my concept of calling them up. When someone is sharing dissatisfaction with us, or when some things need to be corrected, it feels like we're being exposed, uncovered, maybe even shamed (this is being called out). That wasn't what I wanted for my team. I wanted to communicate my support and my desire to elevate their performance which required addressing insufficiencies. That's where calling them up originated. The format that I used when I met with my leader was very similar to the check-in process I used with my staff. We still would go over what they were working on, what was going well, and where they needed support. I asked them about what they had coming up, but what would be different was I would share with them my feedback and observations of them, so they would know what it was that I hadn't seen and what it was that I still wanted to see from them. Then, last but certainly not least, we would talk about what needed to be done by our next check-in, and my check-ins were on a regular schedule. We had a weekly rotation that alternated between team meetings and the individual meetings which allowed me to have weekly touchpoints with my team. Initially, the team was very, very leary of my schedule because they weren't used to having a supportive leader. They were used to punitive meetings with a boss who called them out publicly and privately. They were not accustomed to receiving genuine support. The idea of collaboratively discussing what was happening in their sphere of influence was completely foreign to them. These meetings were designed to provide support and accountability. Ultimately, that is exactly what happened. One of my biggest sources of pleasure and equally my pain point was supervising others and specifically supervising other leaders. These meetings were instrumental in lightening my load while also making a difference for my team. One person with whom I worked had been in the organization for several decades. She literally grew up there, and at the end of our journey she said, "I learned more from you in these last few years than I learned the entire time that I had been here." For me, it made all those one-on-one meetings worth it because not only was I able to help our team meet its goals and supersede them, but also I was able to impact another leader in a life-changing way. Leaders must be critically aware of addressing the missteps in our sphere of influence, whether they are the missteps that we have taken personally or the missteps of our teammates or team members.

In leadership, all the missteps are ultimately your responsibility, which means you take on the brunt of the burden and then distribute the glory. Having this mindset allows you to nurture the morale of your team continuously. This is a privilege that should not be taken for granted or exploited. In many ways, you are responsible for the well-being of others so please handle it with care. To rebuild from defeat, there must be some accountability measures in place. These can be internal/individual or external/team. The scope of these measures truly depends on the size of the comeback. If you are a team of one or an isolated group, setting up internal or individual benchmarks may be enough. However, if you are in need of outside support, or you are connected to a larger dynamic, then external checks and balances may be more appropriate. The purpose is to set you on a path for incremental success and make sure SMART (specific, measurable, attainable, relevant, time-bound) goals are actualized.

Reflection

1. What are the actions, dispositions, or routines that are not serving you well?

2. How are you managing the burden of leading others?

3. On what is your accountability measure based for yourself? For others?

4. What are you doing to be accountable to your leader and hold your team accountable?

5. What needs to happen for you to implement the action items listed below?

_____

_____

_____

_____

_____

_____

_____

_____

_____

Action Items

1. Embrace the weight of leadership. If you don't want to be accountable to or for others, you can't be a leader.

2. Own your imperfections and decide how to address them. Not being accountable will cripple your ability to hold others accountable.

3. Communicate your expectations and hold your team to those expectations. Have a regularly established way to connect with those to whom you are responsible and maintain ongoing communication about their performance.

Evaluation

1. How effective was your implementation of the action items?

2. What more can be done?

3. Is there a more excellent way to operate?

_____

_____

_____

_____

_____

_____

_____

_____

_____

_____

_____

_____

_____

"

LEADERS MUST BE CRITICALLY AWARE OF ADDRESSING THE MISSTEPS IN OUR SPHERE OF INFLUENCE.

CHAPTER 6

Foster Collaboration

No man will make a great leader who wants to do it all himself or to get all the credit for doing it.

- Andrew Carnegie

A s a college professor, I know all too well the disdain that students have for group projects. Whenever I am approached with an objection, I remind students that most of them will be in workplace situations where shared results and teamwork are standard expectations. In school, there is often little choice in how you work together. Professionally, there is a bit more flexibility in the means by which we collaborate, but the fact remains that collaboration is something that is not always enjoyed. Maybe you prefer to work alone. Maybe you have challenging interactions with certain personality types. Maybe you have a way of process that doesn't work well with your colleagues, or maybe you think you can do it all by yourself. No matter what your reason is, collaboration is necessary as a leader. Despite how anyone feels about forced collaboration with colleagues, there is a significant correlation between engagement and organizational performance. Gallup studies show us that higher levels of engagement affect business outcomes such as 41% lower absenteeism, 24% lower turnover, 17% higher productivity, and 21% higher profitability2. These results speak volumes, and these results matter because collaboration is what helps organizations thrive.

Many years ago, when I was a very new leader serving at my church, I learned some critical lessons about collaboration. Although I didn't have a specific role, there were times that I was asked to assist with specific projects for the youth. At the time, the youth had multiple groups that were all operating independently. Occasionally, the autonomy of the groups presented scheduling conflicts and challenges for parents and youth. As a natural organizer, I presented a plan to create one department with multiple components. The goal was to create an umbrella under which all of the existing groups would fall. The biggest problem was that I created the plan in isolation of any of the people who were assigned to lead the groups at the time. Naively, I didn't see the potential roadblocks of the plan, and in all honesty, I didn't even think about being the leader of this proposed union, but that's what ended up happening. We were all in a meeting, and I was announced as the new youth ministry leader. They were told that all these groups were supposed to report to me.

The first problem with this announcement was that no one had a conversation with me prior to this meeting. The second problem was that no one else in the room knew that a proposal had been submitted. Amongst this group of leaders, I wasn't the most qualified, and I definitely was not the most experienced person, but I was the only person who had (presented) a plan. Maybe I was also the only person who even was thinking about bringing all these groups together. This was how they always had operated, and now my plan called for a level of collaboration, which was something to which they were not quite accustomed. My biggest hurdle was navigating the tension between the proposal of collaboration versus their perception of consolidation. This did not go over well. The leaders approached this plan initially as if it was a consolidation. The groups still had the autonomy to operate as they had previously, but they now needed to come together to plan and organize for all the youth. Once they got over their resistance and really understood what was happening, the department started to come up with new ideas and opportunities for the youth. They began to realize the power of working together and combining their strengths and talents. The dance group had lots of energy, but they were poor planners. The choir lacked energy, but they had more parental involvement. The tutoring group had great planners but little excitement or ongoing commitment. When they brought all these things together, it worked masterfully. In fact, it worked just as I had submitted it in the plan.

Effective Teamwork

Understanding and being able to harness the power of collaboration is what causes forward momentum and allows organizations to thrive and to create new ways of being, doing, and operating that truly benefit the end user. What did I learn from this? The first thing I learned from this group was that if they build it, they will grow. When presented with an event or listening to plans, I learned to suppress my ideas to receive input from the team. The alternative to this approach is one that frustrates many people. I'm sure you have been in a conversation with leaders who ask for recommendations, and then they proceed to pick apart and critique every recommendation. This is so easy to do, but it is more damaging than we often realize. It is important that we get feedback from our team members to get their ideas and input, but we must listen to them openly. Many times, once ideas are being shared, the leaders start saying things like, "That won't work." "That's not a good idea." "We've tried that before." "We can't afford that." "We can't do that." "We can't...we can't...we can't." Subconsciously, what gets communicated is "your ideas aren't good enough" and "you are wasting your time." Once this happens, team members stop responding and agree to whatever the leaders say out of obligation, which then produces false collaboration. This diminished participation feels deceptive, and it feels demeaning. Team members who once openly shared ideas that ambitiously contributed to discussions become deflated, and they shrink from participating. They no longer sense a safe place for the exchange of ideas.

Strong teams brainstorm together. They look at a problem, analyze the variables, entertain opposing viewpoints, and finalize options. Giving them the opportunity to share their dream scenarios with a no limits approach and then refining their ideas together invites innovation and creativity. Typically, somewhere between the dream and reality is the solution, the path forward and the progress needed. Unfortunately, if you are shooting down the ideas that are being shared with you and picking apart the brainstorming ideas, you may never get to that. Admittedly, one of the reasons brainstorming doesn't work the way the leader often thinks could be a lack of experience and exposure. Our responsibility as a leader is to make sure we are allowing team members opportunities to be exposed to things outside their department, outside the organization, and outside their small world. When team members are knowledgeable about how other organizations and other industries are doing things, they are able to see that there are other ways to operate. It enlarges their scope and purview of the world, which becomes an asset to the organization. As you grow in sharing ideas and embark on innovating together, delegating becomes increasingly important. When delegating is done well, it is beneficial for all.

Delegating for success is a way of considering strengths and assigning responsibility based on the potential for success. This approach encourages assigning responsibilities based on what people are excited about, as well as what they're good at. That's how you get the most out of people. When you create opportunities for team members to win, you get the most from them. Who doesn't want to be a winner? Who doesn't want to come out on top, and who doesn't want to be amongst other winners? Provide team members this opportunity as you delegate. Don't just give them what you don't want to do, what you don't have time to do, or what you find frustrating. Give them an opportunity to shine, grow, and develop. This also communicates that you believe in them. It says that you see them. It says that you want them to do well, and that type of delegation is going to get them higher on the engagement hierarchy. Leaders who expect collaboration must display a lasting commitment to collaboration (and engagement) by modeling the expectation. To be truly successful, collaboration must be embedded into all levels. Without a doubt, if you're going to lead well, you have to be able to work with all types of people and move them towards a common goal. This movement is necessary even when you don't necessarily agree with them. If you want to make a significant impact, you will need to get past all your objections, preferences, and hang-ups, so you can lead people to work together.

Expansive Network

The organizational chart in and of itself is a tool and a resource that should be used to propel the work forward. Organizational charts aren't just hierarchical diagrams. They also serve as a roadmap of minds, thoughts, insights, and perspectives. As a leader, you need to be able to work effectively and plan strategically with others in the organization. As I was facing my setback, not only could I not be seen talking with other colleagues, but also I was discouraged from closing my office door. It was not a part of the company culture to be interactive and independently collaborative with your colleagues. There were times when the director was seen hovering around open doors or behind walls or lurking to see what others were doing to ensure that conversations were centered around work, and our conversations were kept short. There were times when the director would even walk into a conversation and blatantly ask, "What are you talking about?" The director was just that intent on maintaining full control of everything and everyone in the organization. Not surprisingly, that approach was not only isolating, but it also wasn't useful to working effectively or planning strategically.

Over time, I learned how to navigate this, and I was able to build a network of competent professionals both inside and outside the organization that was able to help with my multi-faceted role. I was responsible for just four staff members, which represented 3% of the organization, and I had an audience of onlookers waiting for my demise. Because that 3% was inextricably connected to every other department within the organization, it was nearly impossible to get anything done without talking to my colleagues. Using my exterior network, I learned enough about the other areas to begin making progress and giving my small but determined team the information necessary to get what they needed within the organization. This strategy actually proved to be extremely beneficial long-term. As a result of this new knowledge, I developed a prowess for navigating federal, state, and local audits without incident or dispute. Criminal allegations and legal occurrences always worked out in our favor, and regulatory agents always were pleased to work with me. This didn't happen easily. It happened because of preparation, determination, and commitment. It happened because of the network I cultivated and the resilience that I displayed in doing what was necessary to understand the work of those around me while figuring out a way to navigate some very challenging conditions. You may not get all the help that you can or would like to have from the organizational chart. You may have to go outside and create your own network until things change.

In the face of defeat, you need your connections. The trick is deciding how to use these connections. Not every connection provides the same benefit. Your task is understanding their role. I recommend categorizing your connection into at least one of these categories: allies, doormen, researchers, enemies, or guardians. Allies are in the trenches working alongside you. Doormen provide access to resources and opportunities. Researchers provide you with information. Enemies are those who create a conflict of interest or are a potential threat to your aspirations. Guardians serve as sounding boards who protect and guide you on your journey. Each of these people has a distinct purpose and each of these people is necessary for your success.

Reflection

1. How good are you at working with others on shared projects?

2. Who is your network to support you, stretch you, and strengthen you?

3. What is your process for delegating tasks?

4. What can you delegate to add to your team's success?

5. What needs to happen for you to implement the action items listed below?

Action Items

1. Create shared opportunities. Give your team something to take ownership of that can further their commitment and ownership.

2. Delegate for success. Avoid assigning tasks based on your individual needs or desires without considering strengths, challenges, and responsibilities.

3. Categorize your connections. This is your external team, and they can be key in your progress.

4. Examine your network. Determine if you are connected to people who will empower, inspire, elevate, and challenge you.

Evaluation

1. How effective was your implementation of the action items?

2. What more can be done?

3. Is there a more excellent way to operate?

_____

_____

_____

_____

_____

_____

_____

_____

_____

_____

_____

_____

IN THE FACE OF DEFEAT, YOU NEED YOUR CONNECTIONS.

PREPARATION FOR NEXT STEPS

Don't show up for the future dressed like yesterday.

Go online to download the
Networking Guide

www.myimpactbook.com/tools

CHAPTER 7

Cultivate Tenacity

"In life and in a boxing ring, the defeat is not declared when you fall down. It is declared only when you refuse to get up."
- Manoj Arora

I n 2015, Time Magazine published an article about contestants competing in the Defense Department's Warrior Games. The 15 remarkable individuals interviewed were all service men and women whose lives and mobility had been altered forever by a significant injury. Generally, the stories were about each veteran's participation in the games. The focus of the interviews was forward-facing and highlighted the joys of the games, not the tragedy of their injuries. The story of Jenae Piper, a retired U.S. Marine Corps Sergeant spoke directly to me. Her account of the games was that the games gave her "a new purpose and the opportunity to set and reach new goals.3 " It amazes me to see people that have figured out how to thrive amidst remarkable physical challenges and limitations. Resilience theory tells us that people utilize a number of internal factors and external supports to thrive in adversity, frustration, and misfortune. The article further stated that the Warrior Game contestants each had in common "the will to overcome—the same will that led them to serve in the first place."

Although I have never had the courage to serve my country as a member of the armed forces, I have faced adversity, frustration and misfortune. For me, these soldiers served as advisors on how to stand tall no matter what setbacks or defeat I might encounter. My distinction between a setback and defeat is the issue of finality. A setback is a trying time or mistake from which you can recover - getting demoted, having a bad evaluation, facing a lawsuit, losing a contract, and dealing with organizational restructuring with the possibility of another position are all examples of setbacks. A defeat is a place when whatever happened severed the opportunity in such a way that returning is not an option - getting terminated, getting laid off with no option of returning, facing a termination of a contract, or receiving a guilty verdict. My defeat came in the form of a layoff, significant restructuring, and relocation all at once. After rebounding from my setback, I was doing very well professionally, but admittedly, I was ready for a change. Little did I know that a change was coming in the form of a layoff. Based on a reduction of funding, the organization went in a different direction, and could no longer sustain a multi-disciplinary executive team. The same organization that was the stage for my setback was now the stage for my defeat. This was a first for me. I was in shock. I felt humiliated. I was afraid. I was unsure of my next steps, and I also felt trapped.

Strong Foundation

My refusal to quit came from an insatiable desire to succeed which was amplified further by attempts to minimize my value. The fighter in me had suited up, and my passion to make a difference for clients and staff was stronger than ever. This determination pushed me to grow where and when it mattered by investing in my development. There were many things that I was forced to learn, numerous places I had to apply research, and multiple places where I needed to develop connections. Developing those connections provided a compass to guide me in the right direction for acquiring much needed knowledge. This compass has to be what guides you. Your environment should not control you. You need to be the one who controls your environment. With increased confidence, I had a sturdy foundation for navigating the traps and barriers set before me. I was able to overcome the constraints that were placed on me. Being forced to figure it out and work on my own made me stronger, more informed, and better equipped. What I didn't know at the time was that it was preparing me for my next chapter. Building your capacity with the right resources and a strong network fortifies your foundation. Part of this process includes having a comprehensive view of your leadership landscape. You first need to be clear on your aspirations and the results you are pursuing. Once you are clear on where you want to land, you need to identify any gaps. An analysis of strengths, weaknesses, opportunities, and threats (SWOT Analysis) will help you to clarify what your needs are and where you can spend your efforts and resources.

Strong Mindset

Your most important resource is your mindset. When faced with setbacks and defeat, persistence and perseverance are necessary to fuel every action and every decision. This will give you the stamina to embrace challenges and persist in the face of innumerable obstacles. When you have the proper mindset, you function as if every obstacle is a mere hurdle that you will conquer. Your focus is always on the finish line, and every adversity becomes a classroom. Adversity can be an incredible incubator for growth. As you grow, you also learn when and how to break the rules or forge a new path. I figured it out. I figured out how to navigate. I figured out how to send emails to the right people. I figured out how to run the reports I needed. I figured out how to read the reports I needed to learn from the system that seemed off limits. I educated myself, so I was effective. Ultimately, what happened is because of strategic thinking, planning, critical thinking, and strategic planning that 3% expanded and became more successful than anyone ever conceived. Ultimately, it became an area in which the rest of the organization was deeply intrigued. In two years, the 3% became 20%, and my responsibility under a new leader soared as I became second in command under a new leader. Although I was in search of a new job during my setback, my tenacity helped me to outlast those who were coming against me. Ultimately, when you are trying to win, there is no time to become trapped in your thoughts or overcome with emotion. Mourn the losses you have and make the decision to fight.

Reflection

1. What does winning look like for you?

2. In what areas do you need to grow?

3. How do you invest in your growth?

4. What needs to happen for you to implement the action items listed below?

Action Items

1. Invest in your growth and development. Knowledge is the foundation of strong decision-making.

2. Maintain agility. Use your knowledge to help maintain flexibility in navigating changing times or pressing demands.

3. Outline your aspirations and results. You need to identify the direction in which you are going to be able to maximize your time, effort, and resources.

4. Conduct a SWOT Analysis. Having this information will allow you to identify any gaps and needs.

Evaluation

1. How effective was your implementation of the action items?

2. What more can be done?

3. Is there a more excellent way to operate?

YOUR ENVIRONMENT SHOULD NOT CONTROL YOU. YOU NEED TO BE THE ONE WHO CONTROLS YOUR ENVIRONMENT.

CHAPTER 8

The Consistency Quandary

Not everything that is faced can be changed, but nothing can be changed until it is faced.

- James A Baldwin.

Without a doubt, three of the most regarded basketball champions of (some would say) all time are Kobe Bryant, LeBron James, and Michael Jordan in alphabetical order. Although their approach may not have been identical, one thing the three of them had in common was their work ethic. Kobe watched footage and practiced incessantly. Lebron developed a comprehensive approach to rest, recovery, training, diet, and lifestyle, while Jordan kept a strict sleep schedule and trained very, very hard. One could argue that their approach was not as important as the cumulative effort of consistent actions that guaranteed their greatness. In fact, that is really why we celebrate longevity and excellence. We celebrate longevity and excellence because it almost always includes an immeasurable consistency that escapes many.

Consistency in both commitment and character have been beneficial for me. It has been the glue that held things together when I faced the most challenging times. Even with this consistency, there are times when I have had to revisit my impact. There are times when I have to refocus and make sure that I haven't lost my foundation. I have had to make sure that I was still building momentum, and I need to ensure that I don't lose sight of my influence. Now that I'm on the other side of the setback, I can tell you that as a result of these things, my scope of responsibility was restored, and I was promoted. I outlasted those who were trying to hold me back - those who had doomed me to fail. Most lasting to me though is the impact I had on the staff. After all of the dust settled, several of them shared that they always looked to me for direction even when others didn't want them to turn to me. When the organization changed directions and had a massive layoff, many made the statement that they wanted to go wherever I was going. Admittedly, after years of not working together, the same people still reach out to me on special occasions, and they championed the launch of my consulting firm. They continue to seek my counsel on career decisions and defer to me in times of crisis. What I learned from all of this is that while consistency communicates commitment, commitment fuels consistency. The two are connected in a dynamic way that cements you in the fabric of any undertaking. My commitment was not only to the work but to the people who did the work. Not only did I prioritize meeting the numbers and hitting the goals, I also prioritized their growth and development. I spent time preparing them for their next level. When you continue to do things in the same way, this becomes both an expectation and your reputation.

Leaders can never lose sight of how important it is for their reputation, values, and actions to align. Consistency in thought, deed, and communication are what it takes to display this level of character. Anything outside this suggests instability and is a threat to trust. Abraham Maslow in his hierarchy of needs shared that one of our basic human needs is safety and security. A duplicitous personality creates an unstable environment for employees and makes them lose sight of their safety and security. They become uptight. Their innovation is stifled, and their confidence is diminished. Teams need their leader to be who the leader that the leader claims to be - the words and action must agree. When your words, actions, and character align, your reputation and results will speak for you in rooms that you may never enter. As important as consistency is, there is another reality.

Consistency with no regard for change invites demise. Successful leaders not only acknowledge that there are times when switching things up is necessary, but they also do not shy away from this necessity. Every change should represent an opportunity for growth or improvement. There is a science to managing change, and good leaders must know how to pivot. Pivoting is essential because it helps you to maintain control. It allows you to stay grounded, and it keeps you from spinning your wheels and wasting time. Commit to being consistent in character and commitment. Be consistent in addressing inconsistent patterns and conquering complacency but avoid the consistency that leads to complacency. Complacency is where you operate as if you have guaranteed success and never need to make progressions or adjustments to maintain relevance. Complacency is a risky place to be. Successful leaders know how to read the times and read their people. This is the skill that allows you to take note of what is going well, yet you are able to make the shifts necessary for continued progress without threatening the ongoing security of team members. When people don't feel safe, they do not perform at optimal levels no matter how hard they try. This isn't a cerebral choice. It is a result of human psychology, a force against which we rarely win. Pay attention to the moves you make, as well as those you don't make as a leader. There is much more at stake than your reputation.

The journey from defeat has made me deeply aware of how powerful we can be as people. Without a doubt, you decide what is on the other side of defeat. Defeat is an invitation for you to define success for yourself. I decided to reintroduce myself, but for some, it may be a realignment, a repositioning, or even a retirement. A realignment allows you to make some adjustments exactly where you are. A repositioning allows you to make needed changes and move into something related. There is no greater sign of the need for change than defeat. Some things need to come to an end. Say goodbye. Mourn the loss and then work on your recovery mission. This was just one battle; you didn't lose the entire war. Every lesson you have learned and every mistake that you made has prepared you for this time. Step into it with all the passion and fire that you can muster knowing that you are on your way to your next season of greatness.

Reflection

1. Where are the inconsistencies in your thoughts, actions, and communication?

2. What consistent pattern do you need to release or revamp?

3. Where are changes necessary in your sphere of influence?

4. What needs to happen for you to implement the action items listed below?

Action Items

1. Identify your priorities. It is necessary to know what is most important, so you are giving your energy to the right things.

2. Determine what efforts you will continue. Your energy and resources are best spent focusing on the things that are in alignment with your priorities. Anything else is likely a distraction.

3. Decide what things are no longer beneficial and need to be eliminated. Be sure to determine what the ripple effects will be, but there is no reason to hold on to things that no longer serve you well.

4. Prepare for the pivots. When something is working well there is no guarantee that it is also working for your benefit. With strong systems and processes in place, disturbances caused by changes are temporary at best. Consider what and where modifications are needed.

Evaluation

1. How effective was your implementation of the action items?
2. What more can be done?
3. Is there a more excellent way to operate?

_____

_____

_____

_____

_____

_____

_____

_____

_____

_____

_____

_____

"

**CONSISTENCY COMMUNICATES
COMMITMENT, COMMITMENT
FUELS CONSISTENCY.**

EPILOGUE

The preceding pages have provided a blueprint for handling any professional setback and making the pivots necessary for ongoing success. Although failures seem to happen in an instant, success takes time to build. To counter-act the speed of the spiral, you need to take action now and create an upward trajectory for yourself. This trajectory is built on a foundation of confidence that is steeped in a track record that you already have. As you conclude this book, I want to provide you with one last thought for each chapter.

Chapter 1/Get to the Bottom of It - Acknowledge your disappointment and identify exactly what is holding you back. Without getting to the root of your setback, you only will deal with the surface issues. True success requires going beyond the surface.

Chapter 2/Respect Your Influence - Use your track records as a launch point for overcoming setbacks.

Chapter 3/Build Momentum - Don't go for the big

wins (yet). Boost your performance with continuous movement and success.

Chapter 4/Solve Their Problems (and Yours too) - Identify ways that you can present solutions or innovations to solve problems.

Chapter 5/Take and Apply Accountability - Starting with yourself, diligently address the missteps in your sphere of influence.

Chapter 6/Foster Collaboration - Build your capacity by connecting with those who can strengthen and inform you in areas where you are deficient.

Chapter 7/Cultivate Tenacity - You have the power to determine what's next. Defeat doesn't have to be the end. You are the one who defines your success.

Chapter 8/The Consistency Quandary - Commit to addressing areas of inconsistency patterns, conquering complacency, and understanding when it is time to move on.

It's time to move forward and make a new mark. Don't let this be the end of your journey. Your past success is more than an indication of what you can do in the future. Your past success is the fuel you need to keep going and growing stronger. Rediscover, reclaim, and reignite your impact and further your leadership legacy!

ENDNOTES

[1] "17 Mind-Blowing Employee Engagement, Performance Review, and Performance Management Statistics," Clear-Company, July 14, 2022, https://blog.clearcompany.com/mind-blowing-statistics-performance-reviews-employee-engagement.

[2] "How to Improve Teamwork Collaboration in the Workplace," Gallup, https://www.gallup.com/cliftonstrengths/en/278225/how-to-improve-teamwork.aspx.

[3] Mandy Oaklander, "Meet 15 Extraordinary Wounded Warriors Who Are Stronger Than Ever,"
TIME magazine, https://time.com/wounded-warriors/.

ABOUT THE AUTHOR

An author, coach, consultant and speaker, Dr. Keena R. Mosley is the Chief Transformation Officer at Momentum Leadership Group - a coaching and consulting firm that provides early education, non-profit, and social service organizations with leadership development solutions to engage their teams, maximize results, and empower middle managers for sustainable success. When not working with current leaders, Dr. Keena serves as a college instructor where she contributes to the development of the next generation of educators. To access more transformational resources, visit www.DrKeena.com.

PROVIDING SOLUTIONS
FOR YOUR
LEADERSHIP PROBLEMS

LEADERSHIP TRANSFORMATION COACHING

A customized in-person experience for individuals or teams

VIRTUAL GROUP COACHING

90-days of leadership coaching with pre-scheduled meetings *(group and individual)*

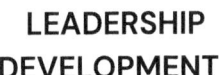

LEADERSHIP DEVELOPMENT

Virtual series or on-site sessions customized to meet the needs o your organization

SELF-DIRECTED COURSES

Multiple topics available including pre-recorded modules and implementation exercises